She
Persisted

DOROTHY HEIGHT

—INSPIRED BY—

She Persisted

by Chelsea Clinton & Alexandra Boiger

DOROTHY HEIGHT

Written by
Kelly Starling Lyons

Interior illustrations by
Gillian Flint

PHILOMEL

☞ *For* ☜

my sorors of Delta Sigma Theta Sorority, Inc.,
and readers everywhere who give from the heart

PHILOMEL
An imprint of Penguin Random House LLC, New York

First published in the United States of America by Philomel,
an imprint of Penguin Random House LLC, 2023

Text copyright © 2023 by Chelsea Clinton.
Illustrations copyright © 2023 by Alexandra Boiger.

Philomel is a registered trademark of Penguin Random House LLC.

Visit us online at PenguinRandomHouse.com.

Library of Congress Cataloging-in-Publication Data is available.

Printed in China

HC ISBN 9780593528976
PB ISBN 9780593528983

2

Edited by Talia Benamy and Jill Santopolo.
Design by Ellice M. Lee.
Text set in LTC Kennerley Pro.

DEAR READER,

As Sally Ride and Marian Wright Edelman both powerfully said, "You can't be what you can't see." When Sally said that, she meant that it was hard to dream of being an astronaut, like she was, or a doctor or an athlete or anything at all if you didn't see someone like you who already had lived that dream. She especially was talking about seeing women in jobs that historically were held by men.

I wrote the first *She Persisted* and the books that came after it because I wanted young girls—and children of all genders—to see women who worked hard to live their dreams. And I wanted all of us to see examples of persistence in the face of different challenges to help inspire us in our own lives.

I'm so thrilled now to partner with a sisterhood of writers to bring longer, more in-depth versions of these stories of women's persistence and achievement to readers. I hope you enjoy these chapter books as much as I do and find them inspiring and empowering.

And remember: If anyone ever tells you no, if anyone ever says your voice isn't important or your dreams are too big, remember these women. They persisted and so should you.

Warmly,
Chelsea Clinton

She
Persisted

DOROTHY HEIGHT

TABLE OF CONTENTS

....

·····························

A Helping Hand

D r. Dorothy Irene Height was always a helper. As a little girl, her mom taught her to never look down on anyone, but to ask herself how she could make their lives better. Dorothy loved finding ways to serve. She gave music lessons to young friends. She helped struggling classmates study. She pitched in wherever needed, just like her parents. Dorothy had no idea that helping would become her life's calling and lift people up around the world.

On March 24, 1912, Dorothy was born into a Virginia community where Black-owned businesses and schools stood proudly. People there worked hard, looked out for each other, and gave back.

Her parents, Fannie Burroughs Height and James Height, welcomed her, their beautiful baby, to a place that held immense promise. But they knew the incredible danger it could pose to a Black child too. Segregated Richmond had different rules for Black and white people. Signs, mean words, and stares let Dorothy's family know where they could go—and where they could not.

In Black neighborhoods like theirs, her family felt seen, loved, and safe. But in others, fairness and freedom could depend on the color of your

skin. Dorothy's parents knew those segregation laws were wrong. Each had been married before and raised children in that environment. They wanted something more for their family.

Four years after Dorothy was born, the Heights moved from the South to the North in search of new opportunities and with the hope of finding less discrimination. From the 1910s to the 1970s, millions of Black people did the same. That movement was called the Great Migration.

Dreams billowed like smoke in the town near Pittsburgh, Pennsylvania, that was their new home. From the whistle of the steel mill to the whoosh of the railroad, Dorothy heard the music of people creating a life. She loved the languages and songs that zigged through evening streets like jazz. She loved the stories of families who'd moved to Rankin, like hers did, for a better chance.

When the US entered World War I, Dorothy's community supported the fight. Some people served in the war. Some worked in the steel mill producing important items like military weapons, helmets, and armor for tanks and ships. The spirit of helping was all around.

Dorothy got along with everyone. She greeted elders as she walked through the neighborhood where a sprinkle of Black migrants from the

South lived side by side with white European immigrants. She was respected by teachers and friends. Her best buddy was her next-door neighbor Sarah, whose family was Irish Catholic. They loved walking to school together and enjoyed special moments like running down a hill, feeling the wind kiss their cheeks. That was one of Dorothy's favorite thrills.

With a flutter of excitement, they would stand at the top of a hill and reach out to each other. They'd smile. Then they'd clasp their hands, Black and white.

One, two, three.

In a flash, the girls flew down the hill as if they had wings. Their feet sailed across the ground as they ran, hand in hand, to the bottom. Breathless, they laughed and climbed the hill again.

But one day, when Dorothy felt that flutter, she reached out her hand and Sarah kept hers right where it was. She called Dorothy a *terrible* word, a word used to hurt Black people, a word so awful, Dorothy's eyes blurred with tears. Devastated, she watched Sarah run down the hill alone.

When her mom returned from work, Dorothy asked her about that *terrible* word. Wrapping Dorothy in her embrace, her mother told her: "She doesn't know who you are."

Dorothy could play with her little sister and other friends, but she never forgot that day with Sarah. A question echoed in her mind: Why did some people say mean things to others just because their skin was a different color?

Dorothy had asked herself tough questions before. When the war ended, jobs at the steel mill became scarcer. Sometimes Dorothy listened to her father and a circle of Black men discussing the situation around the dinner table. Dorothy wondered: Why were Black men the first to be fired? Another time, she heard her mom talking on the phone and a question rose again: Why couldn't her mother, who had been head of nurses at a Black hospital in Richmond, work in a hospital here?

Her family lived in the North, but Black people still faced discrimination, being treated unfairly because of their race. That stuck with Dorothy. But so did the hope that surrounded her every day.

She watched her dad, a talented building contractor and painter, give jobs to men who needed them. She saw her mom find a way to use her nursing skills by caring for patients in their homes. In her parents, she saw models of ways for people to use their gifts to make the world shine. This was something that would guide her throughout her life.

Emerging Leader

In time, Dorothy discovered her own way to make a difference. Though she struggled with asthma so severe, she had to sleep some nights sitting up, Dorothy rarely missed a day at school and earned top grades. She tutored immigrant friends in English. She lit the furnace on frosty Sundays at Emmanuel Baptist Church, where her dad was choirmaster, Sunday school superintendent, and deacon, and she enjoyed being part of the Sunday school and choir. She helped with her little sister, Anthanette, just as her big sisters had helped with her in Richmond. Her parents didn't expect any less.

Weekends, Dorothy would have rather stayed home reading poetry or jumping double Dutch, but her mother took her to meetings of the Federation of Colored Women's Clubs. There, Dorothy listened to messages about being of service to the community, messages that stayed with her long after she was home.

One day, Dorothy watched a wooden building called the Rankin Christian Center being built across the street from her house. Eventually, it transformed into a beautiful brick complex with a chapel, gym, and library. Dorothy was excited to hear it would be open to all. Then she found out what that really meant—six days a week for white immigrants and one day a week for Black people like her.

Every morning, Dorothy would hear the kindergartners in the Christian Center fussing. And every morning, she asked herself: What can you do to help? One day, Dorothy went to see the director, who had become a friend, and offered to read the children Bible stories and teach them songs and plays. Never had a Black girl read to white kids on whites-only days. Ms. Luella Adams said Dorothy would be the first.

On those days, Dorothy sat in the library of the

Christian Center surrounded by eager children who soaked in every word. From the front windows, Dorothy could see her house. She was no longer on the outside looking in. Dorothy was on the inside making a difference.

It was at the Christian Center that Dorothy was invited by two Black sorority women to be a member of the Young Women's Christian Association (YWCA) Girl Reserves, a service organization. She eventually became president of the Rankin chapter and was even picked to be on a poster for the Pittsburgh YWCA.

Twelve-year-old Dorothy and her friends rode the streetcar to the downtown YWCA to celebrate. But when they told the front desk clerk they wanted to learn to swim, the response was: no Negroes allowed.

"I would like to see the executive director," Dorothy said, thinking there was a mistake.

The director was polite but stuck to the rules. Hurt, Dorothy and her friends left. But for a long while after, Dorothy heard a new question calling deep inside: Where was the justice?

Back home in Rankin, Dorothy kept achieving. She played basketball on a high school team with Black and white members. She made straight As in school and was on the debate team. She and a Black friend, Dolly Slaughter, composed the school song. At every assembly, Dolly would play the piano. And, if the music teacher wasn't there, Dorothy would stand on the auditorium platform and lead the class in singing the words she had written.

But then a new principal came who didn't

like a Black girl starting the singing at assemblies.
At the next gathering, he asked Dorothy to sing
with her class instead of going to the stage. When
Dolly started playing, Dorothy stood, but the rest
of her class stayed right where they were. Twice,

Dolly played the first notes of the school song, and twice, Dorothy's classmates refused to budge.

Finally, after Dolly's third try, Principal Straitiff gave up and waved Dorothy to the stage: As soon as Dorothy stood in front of them, the class rose as one.

Dorothy's soprano soared through the auditorium, seasoning the air with its sweetness. It flew as free as the Monongahela River and as high as a mountain.

....

Called to Serve

One day when Dorothy was a high school senior, on her way into a basketball game at the Rankin Christian Center, she noticed a poster promising a $1,000 scholarship to anyone who won a speech-making contest. A champion member of the debate team, Dorothy had already won a different tournament in Harrisburg. But in some ways, this contest—which offered enough money to cover college—was her most important test of all.

Dorothy focused her speech on the Thirteenth, Fourteenth, and Fifteenth Amendments of the Constitution, which guaranteed equal treatment to Americans of all races. A young man who worked for her dad helped her study. Teachers pitched in. Even Principal Straitiff, who had become a cheerleader of her work, called an assembly so classmates could help.

Dorothy won each stage of the competition. Finally, just the national contest in Chicago stood between her and the scholarship. But Dorothy faced a last-minute challenge. She had to cut her twenty-minute speech in half or she would lose.

A teacher had once told her that speeches are not about talking; they're about thinking. Dorothy's mind held so many memories: Sarah

and the hill. Being turned away from the Y. Her
classmates cheering her on.

Dorothy opened her mouth and the answers
to her heart's questions flowed clear as a song.
She spoke words about fairness for all people.

Words about freedom and equality that came out as strong as a choir of voices.

An all-white jury awarded Dorothy the scholarship. And as she looked at the thousands of people witnessing this moment from the audience, Dorothy knew she was right where she was meant to be. Dorothy applied to Barnard College in New York City at the suggestion of her big brother William Briggs. She dreamed of being a psychiatrist, a doctor who helps people with their mental health.

Invited to Barnard for an interview, Dorothy was jumpy but excited. That joy burst like a popped balloon when she spoke with the dean. Dorothy found out that she had been accepted but couldn't attend that fall. The dean said they had already reached their quota of two Black students allowed to attend each year. Dorothy would have to wait until the next year. Where was the fairness? Where was the justice?

Heartbroken, Dorothy persisted. She talked to her big brother again, who suggested she try New York University (NYU). She and her big sister Jessie went to see the dean. Though Dorothy hadn't applied, the dean took one look at her grades and admitted her. Dorothy was on her way.

In the fall of 1929, Dorothy became a freshman at NYU and got right to work. She lived with Jessie and her family, and just like in high school, dedicated herself to studying and helping to create change. Dorothy aced her courses and marched to protest lynchings, which were illegal executions by a mob, and poll taxes, where some people had to pay money to vote in elections. She soaked in the sights and sounds of their Harlem neighborhood. The streets rang with a renaissance of Black creativity. She heard lectures from leading thinkers like W. E. B. DuBois, listened to music with blues pioneer W. C. Handy, enjoyed poetry read by Langston Hughes, and even picked up a side job writing obituaries and proofreading Marcus Garvey's newspaper.

Everywhere Dorothy looked, she saw people making a difference. She earned her bachelor's degree in three years and used the fourth year of her scholarship to earn a master's degree in educational psychology. One of her first professional jobs was at Brownsville Community Center in Brooklyn. While a graduate student, Dorothy helped to manage a team feeding people who were out of work.

It was the Great Depression, a time when many people in the United States and other parts of the world had lost their jobs and their money. Times were tough and people needed a hand. A new dream began to grow in Dorothy's mind. She didn't want to be a doctor. She wanted to help people by serving and making sure they were treated fairly and had what they needed to succeed.

When she finished her studies, the director of the community center arranged a meeting with the board. He hoped to find someone to pay Dorothy's salary so she could stay on full-time. As Dorothy talked about where she grew up, a woman asked if she had heard of the Rankin Christian Center. Dorothy couldn't believe it. Here was someone who had seen her telling Bible stories to immigrant children back home. That woman offered to pay her salary. Dorothy knew she was on the right track.

························

Champion of Rights

Faith in her purpose filled Dorothy with direction and strength. It felt like her life was lining up in divine order. Another job that brought her full circle was working as an assistant executive director for the Harlem branch of the YWCA, the same organization that she had served as a member of the Girl Reserves—and whose downtown Pittsburgh branch wouldn't let her swim. She had the honor of escorting First

Lady Eleanor Roosevelt into a National Council of Negro Women, Inc. (NCNW), meeting that college founder and educator Mary McLeod Bethune was having. Mrs. Roosevelt and Mrs. Bethune took an immediate liking to Dorothy.

Mrs. Roosevelt later invited her to help plan a World Youth Conference and became a cherished friend and example of being an advocate, listener, and leader. Mrs. Bethune, an adviser to President Roosevelt, became an instant mentor. She told Dorothy that NCNW needed her.

"She drew me into her dazzling orbit of people in power and people in poverty . . . 'The freedom gates are half ajar,' she said. 'We must pry them fully open.' I have been committed to the calling ever since," Dorothy shared in her memoir.

Dorothy helped Mrs. Bethune fight against lynching and rally for fairness in hiring and education, and she learned plenty along the way. Any time Mrs. Bethune asked Dorothy to attend a meeting for her, Dorothy was there. She made calls, thought through possible strategies to achieve their goals, shared ideas, and put them into action. Dorothy grew with every lesson.

While working with Mrs. Bethune, Dorothy rose in the ranks of the YWCA. Wearing elegant hats also known as crowns, which would be a trademark throughout her life, she was a groundbreaker whose determination, commitment, and brilliance made a big impression on anyone she met. She pushed to end discrimination and helped to extend the YWCA's work around the world. Eventually, under her leadership, the YWCA became fully integrated. The organization that once turned her away from swimming was now open to all.

Like Mrs. Bethune and the two women who encouraged her back in Rankin to join the YWCA Girl Reserves, Dorothy became a member of Delta Sigma Theta Sorority, Inc., a historically

Black sorority dedicated to sisterhood, scholarship, and service. In 1947, she became the tenth national president, expanding their social action and chapters around the world. Dorothy won lots of respect and admiration, but attention and accolades weren't her focus. What mattered was doing the work.

Ten years later, she became the leader of NCNW, the organization founded by her mentor and inspiration Mrs. Bethune. Dorothy empowered Black women around the nation to advocate for their rights, helping them push for relief from hunger, secure good jobs, and get resources to support their families. While guiding NCNW, she became the only female member of a coalition of civil rights leaders. The guiding voices of that group, which included Dr. Martin Luther King

Jr., A. Philip Randolph, and John Lewis, were known in the press as the Big Six. Dorothy knew that it really should have been the Big Seven.

"And I always laughed because I said, I think since I was the one woman in the group, they didn't count me, so that's how it got to be six, because actually we were seven," she said to Michel Martin of NPR.

She worked just as hard and long as the men did. Her voice mattered. But she was often cropped out of newspaper pictures when they were photographed.

"You will accomplish a great deal if you do not worry about who will get the credit," she once said.

As they planned the 1963 March on Washington to call attention to the need for civil rights for all Americans, Dorothy and others like civil rights leader Dr. Anna Arnold Hedgeman, who played a big role in helping to organize the March, urged that a woman speak at the rally. Though she was a prize-winning public speaker, Dorothy didn't ask to have the honor herself. She would have loved for Dr. Hedgeman or another woman to address the nation in a major way, but other than in powerful songs, few women's voices were heard.

As Dorothy listened to Dr. King's soaring "I Have a Dream" speech, she held her head, adorned with a stylish crown, high. She had suggested that he be the last speaker and have as much time as he needed. His words were profound, brilliant, and uplifting. Dorothy would never forget that women were not treated fairly. But she focused

on the work needed to make that happen in the future.

"If the time is not ripe, we have to ripen the time."

That was something Dorothy said often. Maybe she was thinking it then too. She got that saying from Dr. Benjamin Mays, the president of Morehouse College, who introduced her to Dr. King when he was a teen. At the March, Dorothy savored the meaning of Dr. King's speech and the historic moment. Change would come.

. . . .

Creating a Legacy

As NCNW president, Dorothy made registering voters a priority. It was a freedom that Black people were too often denied through awful tactics like poll taxes and unfair tests designed to make voting harder for Black people, and harassment and violence at the polls when people were trying to vote.

NCNW started a project called Wednesdays in Mississippi, founded by Dorothy and Polly

Cowan, a white civil rights activist and NCNW board member. Black and white middle- and upper-class women from the North would travel to that Southern state each week to try to gain support for voting equality and build bridges between races. It was a dangerous journey. In 1964, less than 10 percent of Black people in Mississippi were registered to vote. Black people who tried to secure that right—or encourage others to vote—could be denied, taunted, beaten, or even killed.

The Northern women that Dorothy and others recruited had to understand what they were going into. They would need to follow the rules of segregation. Black women would stay in Black homes. White women would stay in homes or hotels with people of their race. They couldn't act too friendly in public. The Northern women learned nonviolent resistance in case they got into trouble.

They had secret meetings in the evenings to plan. But one day, they decided to go to a white restaurant. The law had recently changed, and it was legal for Black people to go into white restaurants in Mississippi, but they still weren't welcome. Dorothy sat at a table with a Black colleague and

white ones. The atmosphere around them was tense. White workers glared and grumbled as the women ate. A group of white men began to approach them. Thanks to Black workers who made sure they got to their car safely, they made it out okay. The work was full of danger and close calls, but Dorothy felt it was worth it as under-standing grew and more people became committed to civil rights.

Over the years, Dorothy pioneered other trailblazing efforts like helping struggling families grow gardens and care for pigs so they could make more money to support themselves. She fought against laws aimed at destroying the civil rights achievements she and others had made. She got a statue of her mentor, Mary McLeod Bethune, erected in Lincoln Park, the first memorial to a

Black person or woman in a Washington, DC, public park.

"Every day was a step in carrying out the mission of Mary McLeod Bethune," said Dr. Thelma T. Daley, president of the National Council of Negro Women and a former national president of Delta Sigma Theta Sorority, Inc. "She was greatly influenced by the founder of NCNW."

Black history and tradition mattered to Dorothy. She started a national Black Family Reunion in 1986 on the Washington Mall. Generations came together to share, enjoy each other's company, and salute their heritage. In 1994, President Bill Clinton awarded Dorothy the Presidential Medal of Freedom, the nation's highest civilian honor.

The next year, she spoke at the Million Man

March, one of the largest gatherings in the history of the nation's capital. It was held on the National Mall, just like the 1963 March on Washington.

"I am here, because you are here," she said to the masses who attended to show unity, pride, and strength and to make a difference.

Wearing her trademark crown, Dorothy let everyone know how much they mattered, shared the contributions of Black women, and talked about how Black men and women support each other. Her voice was heard.

And Dorothy wasn't done. Under her leadership, the national headquarters of NCNW moved to 633 Pennsylvania Avenue, between the Capitol and the White House, the first Black organization to be housed in that area. Then Dorothy set a goal to pay off the multimillion-dollar mortgage for the

building they were using. It was a tribute to her mentor, Mrs. Bethune, who believed in bringing women together to accomplish great things.

"We are located along the corridor of power," Dorothy said. "Every person who travels to the White House passes this building. They need to see and know the presence of African American women."

Raising the money would be no easy feat. Dorothy campaigned for donations so they could own the building without any debt. With the help of supporters like Oprah Winfrey, Don King, Coretta Scott King, Dick Gregory, and NCNW members around the nation, she did it. The NCNW headquarters is housed in the Dorothy I. Height Building, named in her honor.

······························

A Beautiful Life

In 2004, Dorothy received the Congressional Gold Medal from President George W. Bush. That year, she also became an honorary alumna of Barnard College, the school that wouldn't allow her to attend in 1929 because of its racist quota. The school had apologized for its actions decades earlier and awarded Dorothy its highest honor, a Medal of Distinction, saluting her outstanding work in civil rights. Making her an honorary

graduate brought more healing.

"This action shows the heart of a great insti-
tution," said Dorothy, who received more than
thirty honorary degrees from universities around
the nation. "It not only reaffirms that I was a

deserving person, it recognizes its old mistake."

Looking back on her life, Dorothy said that error by Barnard College helped set her on the path of fighting injustice. For nearly a century, she advocated for Black people and women of all races. She integrated the YWCA, advised nearly a dozen presidents and world leaders, served as NCNW president for four decades, and received countless honors and awards. She was always there, ready to stand up, serve, and speak out.

She was an honored guest when Barack Obama, the first Black president, laid his hand on a Bible used by Dr. King and took the oath of office in 2009.

"This is real recognition that civil rights was not just what Dr. King dreamed," she said of Obama's inauguration. "But it took a lot of people, a lot of work to make this happen, and they feel part of it."

Dorothy became a cherished part of President Obama's circle, just as she had with past US presidents. She was a welcome and frequent visitor at the White House. She came for special observances like Dr. Martin Luther King Jr. Day. She

visited to offer her thoughts. Her insight and opinion, whether discussing health care or unemployment, counted.

On April 20, 2010, Dorothy died at Howard University Hospital. She was ninety-eight. Her achievements wove together the battle for civil rights and women's rights into a seamless quilt. Having one without the other meant the tapestry was incomplete. People around the nation mourned her passing and celebrated a United States hero's beautiful life.

"For her, her life was about service and giving back," said Alexis Herman, former US Secretary of Labor, special friend and honorary daughter to Dorothy Height. "And she always said it wasn't about the many years of her life, but what she did with it."

Outside Washington National Cathedral, American flags fluttered at half-staff to show respect and mourning. Inside, President Barack Obama stepped to the pulpit facing a patchwork of thousands gathered to say goodbye. Many women wore hats in tribute to the queen who always wore a crown.

"The love in this sanctuary is a testament to . . . a life that changed this country for the better over the course of nearly one century here on Earth," he said.

President Obama called her the godmother of the Civil Rights Movement. The world watched and thanked Dorothy for leading and serving. "When the funeral procession going to Fort Lincoln Cemetery turned onto Bladensburg Road, people lined the street for two to three blocks with homemade signs saying 'Welcome Home, Sister' and 'Well Done, Sister,'" Dr. Daley said. "It's etched in my memory. It was so touching. We can never quantify her reach."

Since Dorothy's passing, there have been exhibits of her hat collection and awards named in her honor. In 2017, her image graced a US Forever postage stamp. Wearing a stylish hat made by one of her favorite hatmakers, Vanilla Beane, Dorothy has a gentle smile and gaze that looks like she's deep in thought or considering something we can't see.

In many ways, Dr. Dorothy Irene Height is still with us. Her work lives on in millions of children like you. Remember her, and dream not just of what you will do when you grow up but of the kind of person you will be.

HOW YOU CAN PERSIST

by Kelly Starling Lyons

Ever since she was a child, Dr. Dorothy I. Height found her way to make a difference. You can too. Here are some tips from her life:

1. Find your purpose. What is your passion? How can you help the world shine brighter? Volunteer, participate in activities, look within and ask yourself

what lights a spark in your heart.

2. Help and lead. Part of leading is serving. When you join a club or cause, pitch in wherever you can and offer to be in charge when you can make a difference. Be confident, collaborate, and show commitment to your goal.

3. Stand up for change. Remember that you matter. Hold your head high and use your voice to make your feelings known. If you see something wrong, say something. Speak loud and proud and push for justice. You can write letters to your elected officials or local newspapers to express your opinion or encourage change; march in a protest with a parent, caregiver, or trusted

adult; or create art, essays, or poems that share your point of view.

4. Work together. Find people who share your purpose and unite. A movement starts with one person who wants to make a difference. Joining with others gives you strength, momentum, and power.

5. Be prepared. Spend time researching causes you care about. Study history and what's happening today. Doing your homework means you're ready for anything.

6. Honor your elders. Dorothy's heroes included her mother, college founder and educator Mary McLeod Bethune, and First Lady Eleanor Roosevelt.

They taught her the importance of being generous, humble, and dedicated to making life better for all.

7. Persevere and have faith. You're going to face challenges in life. It's how you deal with them that counts. Hold on to hope and press on. Think about inspiring changemakers like Dr. Height if you feel doubt creeping in. You can do anything as long as you believe.

ACKNOWLEDGMENTS

Growing up in Pittsburgh, I took pride in our hometown heroes. From pianist Mary Lou Williams and pioneering publisher and editor Robert L. Vann to celebrated playwright August Wilson and super-model Naomi Sims, countless people who made a difference walked the same streets I did. But though Dr. Dorothy Irene Height came of age in Rankin, just a twenty-minute drive from my Beechview neighborhood, I didn't learn her name until college. She was the tenth national president of Delta Sigma Theta Sorority, Inc., the sisterhood I proudly joined. As I read about her life, I was inspired, but felt cheated too. Why hadn't we studied her in school?

Dr. Height created change in so many profound ways. She led the integration of the YWCA. She championed voting rights. She was the president of national women's organizations and a key orga-nizer during the Civil Rights Movement. She advised nearly a dozen presidents. I promised myself that I'd tell her story so that my chil-dren and kids everywhere would know what she achieved—and that they could accomplish anything too. What a blessing to have this opportunity.

Thank you to Chelsea Clinton for creating this inspiring series and giving me and other writers the chance to pay homage to hero-ines who deserve to have their stories known. Thank you to editors Jill Santopolo and Talia Benamy for the gift of choosing me to write this book about Dr. Dorothy I. Height and guiding me along the way. So many people made this book possible. I'm grateful to illustrators Alexandra Boiger and Gillian Flint, the team at Philomel, and my agent, Caryn Wiseman.

Part of the magic of writing is that seeds of stories are planted before you even compose a word. Hugs and love to the chapter where I became a Delta, Kappa Lambda, and to my beautiful sisters of Shinda Shindana, with a special tribute of thanks to Shikilia. As I bloomed into an author, I've had so many people cheering me on. Deep gratitude to the loved ones who kept encouraging me as I dreamed of having a book about Dr. Height: my mom; sister-friends Judy Allen Dodson, Olugbemisola Rhuday-Perkovich, Vanesse Lloyd-Sgambati, and Susan Taylor; and sorors Carole Boston Weatherford, Dr. Pauletta Brown Bracy, Shamara Ray, Carleen Lyken, Kimberly Wilson, Shelia Reich, Stephanie Perry Moore, Dr. Nancy Tolson, and Gwendolyn Hooks. And a bouquet of flowers and thank-yous to Soror Dr. Thelma T. Daley for her kindness, amazing insight, and feedback.

I never had the honor of meeting my incredible soror Dr. Height, but I was in the crowd when she spoke at the Million Man March. As her voice echoed across the Washington Mall, I knew I was in the presence of greatness.

May her beautiful legacy live on.

☙ References ❧

BOOKS:

Height, Dorothy I. *Living with Purpose: An Activist's Guide to Listening, Learning and Leading.* Washington, DC: Dorothy I. Height Education Foundation, 2012.

Height, Dorothy. *Open Wide the Freedom Gates: A Memoir.* New York: Public Affairs, 2003.

ARTICLES, BLOGS, PAPERS, AND TRANSCRIPTS:

Associated Press. "Dorothy Height, Civil Rights Activist, Dies at 98." *Pittsburgh Post-Gazette.* April 20, 2010. post-gazette.com/local/east/2010/04/20/Dorothy-Height-civil-rights-activist-dies-at-98/stories/201004200160.

Associated Press. "Barnard College Honors Pioneer in Civil Rights." *Lewiston Sun Journal.* June 5, 2004. sunjournal.com/2004/06/05barnard-college-honors-pioneer-civil-rights.

Bloom, Linda. "Lowery, Height Join Those on Inaugural Platform." *UM News.* January 20, 2009. umnews.org/en/news/lowery-height-join-those-on-inaugural-platform.

Fox, Margalit. "Dorothy Height, Largely Unsung
    Giant of the Civil Rights Era, Dies at 98."
    New York Times. April 20, 2010. nytimes
    .com/2010/04/21/us/21height.html.

Howard University News Service. "Reaching
    New Heights: NCNW Founder Shares
    Wisdom with Honor Students." hunewsservice
    .com/news/reaching-new-heights.

Lamb, Brian. "Open Wide the Freedom Gates:
    A Memoir by Dorothy Height." C-Span
    Booknotes Transcript. June 24, 2003. c-span
    .org/video/?177169-1/open-wide-freedom
    -gates-memoir.

Leffler, Phyllis, and Julian Bond. "Explorations
    in Black Leadership." UVA Arts & Sciences.
    blackleadership.virginia.edu/transcript/height
    -dorothy.

Martin, Michel. "Civil Rights Elder Sees Dream Come True." NPR Transcript. November 6, 2008. npr.org/templates/story /story.php?storyId=96694471.

Patton, Stacey Pamela. "A Drive to Secure a Piece of History." *Washington Post*. June 29, 2000. washingtonpost.com/archive/local/2000 /06/29/a-drive-to-secure-a-piece-of-history /913ccfc2-450d-43d1-af4e-aa2f5ad8de17.

Rodgers-Melnick, Ann. "Rights 'Queen' Honored Where It All Began." *Pittsburgh Post-Gazette*. July 30, 2003. old.post-gazette .com/localnews/20030730height0730p2.asp.

Smith College. "Dorothy Irene Height Papers." Identifier: SSC-MS-00606. Sophia Smith Collection of Women's History. findingaids .smith.edu/repositories/2/resources/814.

VIDEO:

"User Clip: Dorothy Height." C-SPAN, October 16, 1995. Video, 9:27. c-span.org /video/?c4634598/user-clip-dorothy-height.

PRESS RELEASE:

"Remarks by the President at Funeral Service for Dr. Dorothy Height." Office of the Press Secretary, The White House. April 29, 2010. obamawhitehouse.archives.gov/realitycheck /the-press-office/remarks-president-funeral -service-dr-dorothy-height.

KELLY STARLING LYONS is a founding member of the Brown Bookshelf, a teaching artist, and an award-winning children's book author. Her mission is to center Black heroes, celebrate family, friendship, and heritage, and show all kids the stories they hold inside. Many of her books have won accolades, including a Caldecott Honor for *Going Down Home with Daddy*, a Geisel Honor for *Ty's Travels: Zip, Zoom*, a Christopher Award for *Tiara's Hat Parade*, and a Bank Street Best list for *Sing a Song: How "Lift Every Voice & Sing" Inspired Generations*. She's the author of more than two dozen titles for young readers, including *She Persisted: Coretta Scott King* and the popular Jada Jones series.

You can visit Kelly Starling Lyons online at
kellystarlinglyons.com
and follow her on Twitter
@KelStarLy

GILLIAN FLINT has worked as a professional illustrator since earning an animation and illustration degree in 2003. Her work has since been published in the UK, USA and Australia. In her spare time, Gillian enjoys reading, spending time with her family and puttering about in the garden on sunny days. She lives in the northwest of England.

You can visit Gillian Flint online at
gillianflint.com
or follow her on Twitter
@GillianFlint
and on Instagram
@gillianflint_illustration

CHELSEA CLINTON is the author of the #1 *New York Times* bestseller *She Persisted: 13 American Women Who Changed the World*; *She Persisted Around the World: 13 Women Who Changed History*; *She Persisted in Sports: American Olympians Who Changed the Game*; *Don't Let Them Disappear: 12 Endangered Species Across the Globe*; *It's Your World: Get Informed, Get Inspired & Get Going!*; *Start Now!: You Can Make a Difference*; with Hillary Clinton, *Grandma's Gardens* and *Gutsy Women*; and, with Devi Sridhar, *Governing Global Health: Who Runs the World and Why?* She is also the Vice Chair of the Clinton Foundation, where she works on many initiatives, including those that help empower the next generation of leaders. She lives in New York City with her husband, Marc, their children and their dog, Soren.

You can follow Chelsea Clinton on Twitter
@ChelseaClinton
or on Facebook at
facebook.com/chelseaclinton

ALEXANDRA BOIGER has illustrated nearly twenty picture books, including the She Persisted books by Chelsea Clinton; the popular Tallulah series by Marilyn Singer; and the Max and Marla books, which she also wrote. Originally from Munich, Germany, she now lives outside of San Francisco, California, with her husband, Andrea, daughter, Vanessa, and two cats, Luiso and Winter.

Photo credit: *Vanessa Blasich*

You can visit Alexandra Boiger online at
alexandraboiger.com
or follow her on Instagram
@alexandra_boiger

Read about more inspiring women in the

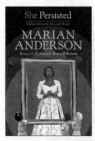

She Persisted
Chelsea Clinton & Alexandra Boiger
MARIAN ANDERSON
Written by Katheryn Russell-Brown

She Persisted
Chelsea Clinton & Alexandra Boiger
VIRGINIA APGAR
Written by Dr. Sayantani DasGupta

She Persisted
Chelsea Clinton & Alexandra Boiger
PURA BELPRÉ
Written by Meg Medina with Marilisa Jiménez García

She Persisted
Chelsea Clinton & Alexandra Boiger
SIMONE BILES
Written by Kekla Magoon

She Persisted
Chelsea Clinton & Alexandra Boiger
ELLA FITZGERALD
Written by Andrea Davis Pinkney

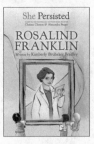

She Persisted
Chelsea Clinton & Alexandra Boiger
ROSALIND FRANKLIN
Written by Kimberly Brubaker Bradley

She Persisted
Chelsea Clinton & Alexandra Boiger
TEMPLE GRANDIN
Written by Lyn Miller-Lachmann

She Persisted
Chelsea Clinton & Alexandra Boiger
DEB HAALAND
Written by Laurel Goodluck

She Persisted
Chelsea Clinton & Alexandra Boiger
CORETTA SCOTT KING
Written by Kelly Starling Lyons

She Persisted
Chelsea Clinton & Alexandra Boiger
CLARA LEMLICH
Written by Deborah Heiligman

She Persisted
Chelsea Clinton & Alexandra Boiger
RACHEL LEVINE
Written by Lisa Bunker

She Persisted
Chelsea Clinton & Alexandra Boiger
MAYA LIN
Written by Grace Lin

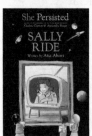

She Persisted
Chelsea Clinton & Alexandra Boiger
SALLY RIDE
Written by Atia Abawi

She Persisted
Chelsea Clinton & Alexandra Boiger
MARGARET CHASE SMITH
Written by Ruby Shamir

She Persisted
Chelsea Clinton & Alexandra Boiger
SONIA SOTOMAYOR
Written by Meg Medina

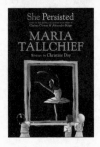

She Persisted
Chelsea Clinton & Alexandra Boiger
MARIA TALLCHIEF
Written by Christine Day

She Persisted series!

She Persisted
NELLIE BLY
Written by Michelle Knudsen

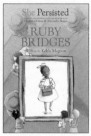

She Persisted
RUBY BRIDGES
Written by Kekla Magoon

She Persisted
KALPANA CHAWLA
Written by Raakhee Mirchandani

She Persisted
CLAUDETTE COLVIN
Written by Lesa Cline-Ransome

She Persisted
BETHANY HAMILTON
Written by Maryann Cocca-Leffler

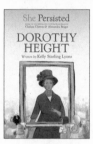

She Persisted
DOROTHY HEIGHT
Written by Kelly Starling Lyons

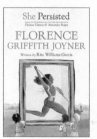

She Persisted
FLORENCE GRIFFITH JOYNER
Written by Rita Williams-Garcia

She Persisted
HELEN KELLER
Written by Courtney Sheinmel

She Persisted
WANGARI MAATHAI
Written by Eucabeth Odhiambo

She Persisted
WILMA MANKILLER
Written by Traci Sorell

She Persisted
PATSY MINK
Written by Tae Keller

She Persisted
FLORENCE NIGHTINGALE
Written by Shelli R. Johannes

She Persisted
DIANA TAURASI
Written by Monica Brown

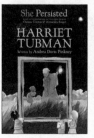

She Persisted
HARRIET TUBMAN
Written by Andrea Davis Pinkney

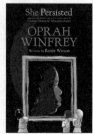

She Persisted
OPRAH WINFREY
Written by Renée Watson

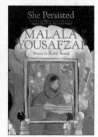

She Persisted
MALALA YOUSAFZAI
Written by Aisha Saeed